*The Most Powerful Words on the Planet,*

# "I Know You Love Me
### and
# You Know I Love You"

## Fulfill the Promise of Your
## Marriage Vows

### by

### Stefan Deutsch

# Acknowledgements

This book is the culmination of my lifelong search for answers about man's inhumanity to man and what I can do about it. As such, it has been a labor of love. There were many times when I wondered, "What am I doing, trying to heal the world?" The answer was always the same: that is what I was given to do and I must proceed.

I want to acknowledge my many clients, everyone who has attended a workshop or lecture, or listened to my radio program. It was your continual enthusiasm for what you learned and the amazing results you achieved that motivated me to carry on writing.

I want to give a special thanks to my wife, who has patiently listened to my ideas about love and human development and supported them for decades. Turning our home into an office and infringing on her privacy was a huge sacrifice, but she allowed me to make this part of my journey easier.

I also want to acknowledge Dr. Roberta Karant, my rock, who steadfastly declared that these concepts and the work they generated were important, and that sooner or later the world would recognize and begin employing them in psychotherapy, marriage, aging, parenting, education, staff development, and beyond.

My final acknowledgment goes to the dozens of volunteers and interns who have worked so hard to bring my ideas to life in our many programs. Amongst them I want to especially thank my editor Emily Wilson, who has patiently and intelligently guided the process of writing this book.

# Contents

# Introduction

# Love's New Possibilities

The three happiest days of my life were when my daughter was born, the day I married my wife, and the birth of my granddaughter. The saddest days of my life have been when loved ones passed away, or when friends and family struggled through divorce and separation. Each event either brought more love into my life or left me with less. That's why I'm thrilled to offer you a book that I'm confident will safeguard the love you have and empower you to strengthen and deepen it even more, making it enduring and unshakable.

Over the last 30 years, I have helped countless people with their relationships. My work with individuals and couples has been very successful, and my presentations at major conferences are always well received. Despite this success, I resisted compiling my theories of love and human development into a book because I did not have hard scientific evidence to support my central thesis that love is vital nourishment.

In 2013, that completely changed. An eight-year scientific study conducted by Dr. Barbara Fredrickson published its findings that, just as

I predicted years before, love is in fact nourishment. I encourage you to learn more about Dr. Fredrickson's scientific findings. If you picked up this book because you want to improve your life and your marriage, just give the concepts and exercises a try and see for yourself how their practical applications transform your marriage.

It is important to point out that your habits are deeply ingrained, and the actions and reactions that have been repeated over a lifetime will take time to unlearn. Ask yourself this question: "Is my happiness and that of those I love worth dedicating some time and effort?"

The ideas and exercises in this book will make an immediate difference, but the deeper, life-changing results that come from mastering a new approach to love and behavior take some time. Patience and persistence are the keys to the kingdom.

## A Recipe for Reading Together

I designed this book to be read by couples together as a relationship enrichment guide. Learning new ideas and approaches to relationships is a wonderful bonding experience, and reading together ensures you'll be on the same page when trying the exercises.

- Learning what love is together will help each of you give it consistently.
- Understanding why being deprived of love causes pain will help you avoid unloving behaviors.
- Rediscovering your lovable qualities and those of your spouse will help you better appreciate each other.
- Writing a relationship vision for the first time together gets any unspoken expectations and anxieties intothe open and will establish that you are a team, in full control over the direction and quality of your marriage.

- Practicing communication and listening exercises together will make you more compassionate when communicating about difficult or emotionally-charged topics.

These rich learning experiences develop the all-important trust that your spouse is just as committed and willing to work at the relationship as you are.

However, many of you may be reading this book on your own. I've found that in many relationships one partner will be interested in books on love, marriage or relationships and personal enrichment workshops or seminars, whereas the other always declines invitations to read or participate. So, whoever has read or heard a tip or tidbit on relationships will try and remember it and give a faithful account. Not surprisingly, most of what catches his/her attention relates to something his/her spouse is doing wrong. Pretty soon the other person picks up on this and starts to feel lectured to, and it all falls on deaf or exasperated ears. Defenses go up, loving communication ends, and an argument can break out—even if the other person realizes there is some truth to what is being shared. Why should s/he listen to criticism disguised as information? Even if the original intention to enrich the marriage is good, instead of reporting on what you read or heard, it is always better to model it yourself.

I want to give you some pointers on how to avoid these thorny areas and inspire your significant other to read the book with you. After all, discovering new concepts and skills together creates a new bond and reinforces the feeling that you're in it together. You both want this marriage to be successful, loving and fulfilling, and are willing to put forth the required effort. Here's an example of a possible dialogue you can have with your partner about reading this book together:

"Hon, there is something I would like for us to read together. Is this a good time to discuss it?" (If yes, proceed; if no, ask when a better time might be.) "I love you and I know you love me. We're a pretty typical couple, and although we have our moments, we make an effort to be respectful, understanding and supportive of one another. We get along and have fun together. I have a feeling that you may not be particularly interested in reading this book with me, but I would really appreciate it if you would try. I think it's important; I think it will be fun; and most importantly I think it will bring us even closer together. We never went to relationship school, so we've been flying by the seat of our pants. We've done pretty well, but I think the ideas in this book will help strengthen our marriage even more. There are few simple exercises that will be fun to do together. What do you say?"

If your spouse refuses, make sure you don't start an argument. Say something like, "Hon, I am disappointed since I had my heart set on reading it together, but I am not angry. Let me know if you change your mind."

If you find yourself reading this book alone, I challenge you to resist playing the role of teacher to your spouse. Instead of trying to share your new knowledge, see if you can model what you're learning. Become more aware of your own unloving behaviors, learn to apologize more readily, be more patient and understanding. In most cases, your new outlook and approach will start to positively influence your spouse's behavior. In a few months, you can make the offer again.

Print this document and post it near your bed. Each truth allows couples to be inspired to grow closer together. Enjoy The Love.

# 13 Truths that Fulfill the Promise of Marriage

1. Love that has to be earned isn't love.
2. Become aware of your own and others' conditional and unconditional behavior.
3. Never reject someone's loving energy; it hurts them when you do.
4. Never allow another to behave unlovingly; it hurts you when they do.
5. Ask others to love you unconditionally. You deserve it like you deserve your next breath – and give it, because so do they.
6. Do not assume that there is any intentionality behind any act that hurts, disappoints, or angers you. Resist the temptation to blame others or assume their actions are designed to hurt you.
7. Assume that everyone is always doing the very best they can, just as you are.
8. Remember that everyone needs the life-sustaining energy of love.
9. Love is cyclical: we need to give it as much as we need to receive it.
10. Loving energy has many names: compassion, patience, acceptance, kindness, generosity, encouragement, affection, consideration, thoughtfulness, etc. – and you need to give and receive every one of these in every one of your relationships, not just a few.
11. The act of giving love involves a conscious decision to be unconditionally loving with another person. You make the choice.
12. Loving energy is not automatic, biological, or procreative. It is not to be confused with physical arousal, fast heartbeats, or sweaty palms. Those are biological signals for mating.
13. Loving energy is real, nourishing, and visceral. It allows us to thrive. Without it we feel empty, lonely, tired, etc. It is exactly like air, food, and water: never to be withheld, especially from yourself.

# Chapter 1
# Why Do We Need Love to Thrive?

Marriage can be the ultimate showcase for the incredible power of unconditional love. Imagine describing your marriage in this way:

> We're two people who have, at the deepest level of our beings, a feeling of peace and serenity. We feel respected, accepted, appreciated, nurtured, and encouraged by each other, safe to say whatever we feel, and enjoy communicating even about difficult topics where we don't see eye to eye. We are affectionate and considerate and have a tranquil family environment full of compassion and understanding.

This is possible only when spouses are able to love each other unconditionally, and the result is incredibly joyful! I've seen it happen time and again with my clients: reframing their ideas of what love is and why they need it shifts their approach to relationships 180 degrees. We need to receive love consistently and unconditionally to experience true happiness, wholeness, and fulfilling relationships. When you're starved for love, your ability to make good decisions for yourself and your relationship is compromised. That is why the first order of business is learning how to love yourself. That is the foundation for giving love and being able to do so unconditionally, creating close, loving relationships. When our need for love is fully satisfied, we feel a balanced sense of tranquility or contentment that simultaneously revitalizes us. We thrive and can become the individuals we were always meant to be.

## Three Square Meals of Love

Understanding the true nature of love is the first step to learning how to give and receive it freely and without condition. After all, love doesn't come wrapped in a cute little package we can simply hand over to one another like a birthday gift. Have you ever asked yourself what love is? Perhaps not, since we all believe we know what love is. We know what we experience; this powerful energy is felt in every cell of our bodies. We translate these feelings using words like "happiness," and "warmth," as well as "pain," "lethargy," "heartache," and "depression," when we are deprived of it. These are descriptive terms about how love makes us feel—not what it actually is.

Like plants turning to face the sun, human beings are drawn to those who warm them with their love. The warmth that comes from most people some of the time and a few people all of the time—their acceptance, generosity, affection, compassion, appreciation, and so on—nurtures and feeds us. When we receive the life sustaining energies in air, food and water we thrive and feel energized, but when we are deprived of them, we experience physical pain and can even die. Similarly, when we receive loving energy we also thrive and feel energized, but when we are deprived of love we experience pain, to the point that some people feel they want to die. I wondered, "Could it be that love also contains a life-sustaining energy? An energy that makes us feel like we're raring to go, or when we don't get it, feel like we can't get out of bed?" If that were true, it would explain why so many of us are desperate for love.

The more I studied our collective experience with love, the more I became convinced that the desperation we feel when looking for love was like the distress people feel when starving or dying of thirst. **I offer a new classification of love as an energy that nourishes and energizes us—an energy that we can get from another person, spouse or stranger alike, and also give to ourselves.**

I have explained to you love is an energy that behaves very much like the life-sustaining energies in air, food, and water. Besides obtaining and ingesting these life-sustaining energies, what else must we do? If you only ate, drank, and inhaled, would that be healthy for you? I know this can sound like a trick question, so I will elaborate. Life-sustaining energies have a common quality: they are cyclical. That means for us to be healthy and have optimum energy we must eat and drink—and expel. We must inhale and exhale. Love has the same cyclical nature. Realizing that we need to give love as much as we need to receive it is vital to our emotional and physical health.

## Can We Learn to Love Unconditionally?

Think of yourself for a moment as an electric generator that can be switched on or off. When we generate loving energy, the switch is activated by our conscious or subconscious thoughts. Most of us turn it on when we feel positively towards a person and turn it off when someone upsets us. Both our negative and positive reactions are mostly automatic. The key is to learn to consciously turn the generator on and keep our hands off the switch even when we're upset.

We all need a consistent supply of nourishing love, given and received unconditionally; and we need it from ourselves as much or more than we need it from others.

- Unconditional love is the conscious choice to both give and accept love consistently, even under painful, upsetting and disappointing circumstances.

- Conditional love gives and accepts loving energy only when you are pleased with someone you're in a relationship with, rather than under any and all circumstances.

During conflicts, loving energy is often either consciously or unconsciously withheld. When we're upset, we don't want others to try to be nice or in any way convince us to stop punishing them until we're good and ready. Even if someone apologizes, we often reject it because we don't believe they've "served their sentence." As I've mentioned, unconditional love requires us to receive and give our love consistently, even in the face of conflict, hurt and anger. But this is very important: it does not require us to deny or disregard our hurt and anger or the behavior that caused it. Big difference! We can acknowledge hurt and confront unloving behavior while still loving the other person.

My father was a very honest, helpful, hardworking man. He would come home and give me a big, sloppy kiss. But he also had a temper and would immediately raise his voice. I absolutely detested it. The older I got, the more I resented the yelling, and did not want him even to come near me. His conditional behavior made me completely turn the switch off. I did not feel any affection for him, nor did I want any from him.

It wasn't until I got married and had a child of my own that I started to forgive him. He also started to view me as an adult and stopped yelling at me, which helped. Eventually, I figured out how incredibly painful losing his parents and siblings in the war had to be for him and started to appreciate that he was a human being who needed love. I recognized that he was doing his best, giving as much love as he could and still needing and deserving love from others, even though his behavior was conditional.

It might surprise you to learn that your ability to be unconditional makes you very powerful. People think if they are unconditional other people will only take advantage of them, but loving unconditionally does not mean just being nice or forgiving other people's mistakes—it means being powerful. It actually creates a great deal of respect, admiration, and even awe for you as other people realize they cannot affect you negatively.

Unconditional love is not synonymous with weakness, dependency, or need, but rather comes from a cultivated inner strength—and therefore it's not something that can be taken advantage of. As a matter of fact, someone who has cultivated the strength to stay loving under difficult circumstances also has the strength to say, "This is not acceptable, and _____ will be the consequence if it doesn't stop," under the same circumstances. Remember, the greatest power human beings have is the ability to love, inspire, and motivate others.

Learning to love unconditionally takes dedication and a willingness to step outside your comfort zone. I promise you it will be worth it. Take a few moments now to commit to loving yourself and your spouse unconditionally, and learning the tools that will help you to realize the incredible power of loving energy in your marriage. I encourage you and your spouse to complete the personal pledges on the following pages, demonstrating your dedication to unconditionally love yourselves and each other.

# PERSONAL LOVE CONTRACT

I, _____, pledge to give myself and my spouse, _____, unconditional love, even during times of conflict and disagreement. Although I may be angry, hurt, or upset, I pledge to express my feelings with love.

I know that an important part of loving myself is to only accept loving behavior from others, including my spouse. Loving myself and others unconditionally makes me powerful, and my loving behavior will help inspire others to grow and become more unconditionally loving themselves.

I understand that this is a process that will take time, and that loving unconditionally means being patient and persistent with myself and others. I am committed to mastering the tools of awareness, vision and compassionate communication in order to love my spouse unconditionally and make our marriage as strong, nurturing and fulfilling as it can be.

SIGNED _____

DATE _____

# Personal Love Contract

I, _____, pledge to give myself and my spouse, _____, unconditional love, even during times of conflict and disagreement. Although I may be angry, hurt, or upset, I pledge to express my feelings with love.

I know that an important part of loving myself is to only accept loving behavior from others, including my spouse. Loving myself and others unconditionally makes me powerful, and my loving behavior will help inspire others to grow and become more unconditionally loving themselves.

I understand that this is a process that will take time, and that loving unconditionally means being patient and persistent with myself and others. I am committed to mastering the tools of awareness, vision and compassionate communication in order to love my spouse unconditionally and make our marriage as strong, nurturing and fulfilling as it can be.

Signed _____

Date _____

# Chapter 2
# Self-Love: The Elixir for Strong Marriages

We all want loving relationships, most of all with our spouses. But you can't love your spouse until you love your Self, which means knowing your Self, embracing your strengths, weaknesses, and needs, and making sure they are being met. People tend to treat us as we treat ourselves, so if you don't love yourself, guess how you will be treated?

When Julie and Martin came to work with me they had already seen a number of therapists and a divorce attorney. There was very little respect and zero communication. They were exhausted by the impasse in the relationship. It was clear they were neither getting nor giving love to each other, nor did they love themselves very much. I asked them to each make a list of their lovable qualities. Julie said she had none, but proceeded to write down three. Martin insisted he had none, and wrote none.

Their homework was to ask friends and relatives to add to their list. The following week Julie came in with tears in her eyes. She had felt all her life that her dad did not love her. She sent him the list anyway and he sent it back with lots of lovable qualities she didn't think she had, but even more significantly, didn't think he saw in her. As a result, her relationship with herself and others improved. She tried to have Martin add to her list, and tried to add to his, but he would not share anything with her.

Martin, who refused to write any lovable qualities down, had nothing to approach friends and relatives with and refused to participate. Consequently he was not able to get any positive feedback and was stuck disliking himself, which caused him to struggle giving or accepting Julie's love. In spite of trying to be supportive and patient, not surprisingly, Julie gave up trying to save their marriage.

## Do You Deserve Three Meals a Day?

In our culture the phrase "love yourself" often conjures up the image of a selfish, self-centered, self-indulgent person. But selfish people only ask for help and are reluctant to give it; spend money on themselves but are stingy with others; always demand love without always reciprocating. Loving yourself couldn't be farther from that negative concept. But it also isn't someone who always says yes, constantly giving of him/herself without ever wanting or asking for anything from others. This "unselfish" attitude usually comes from feeling undeserving of love and support and results in people feeling used and unappreciated. In truth, loving oneself has more to do with how we approach our relationship with ourselves than what we do or ask for from others.

Think of how lovingly you treat your best friend: with respect, appreciation, acceptance, encouragement, support, kindness, patience and compassion. The key is to apply that to yourself. Accept your weaknesses, appreciate your strengths, acknowledge that you are doing your best, and forgive yourself when you make mistakes. When we independently provide nourishing love to ourselves, we become our own best friends. As we can and want to bond with others, so we want and need to bond with ourselves.

Easier said than done? One of the first things you need to do to start on this path is to notice that there is a little voice in your head that is constantly talking. Raising and educating children is almost entirely focused on teaching new concepts and behaviors, which involves a constant stream of correction. Eventually a child starts to internalize that critical voice and hears his or her own constant stream of self-correction. We become so used to it that we often don't even realize we're having a full-blown conversation with our inner selves. That little voice doesn't usually have many complimentary things to say to us, but plenty of critical, unkind things to say. If you believe everything it says it is difficult to even like yourself, never mind love yourself.

Why would we treat ourselves this way? It's simple: there's no risk of losing a relationship with ourselves. We don't have to worry about getting the pink slip or being shown the door: no matter how poorly we treat ourselves, we're stuck with ourselves. This is the same reason that children and spouses sometimes behave unlovingly: they're confident that they won't be fired.

As loud as the impatient, self-defeating voice in your brain can be and as soft as the encouraging signals are at first, the good news is *you* have the power to decide which to listen to. When the negative self-talk starts blaring, choose to switch the channel to the positive signal. Tell yourself that your endeavor will succeed, that your partner or friend will respond to your loving and persistent, positive approach. Say to yourself, "I know I can do this if I am patient with myself."

## Make Unloving Behaviors a Thing of the Past

Make a list of unloving behaviors you have a propensity to apply to yourself. Do you procrastinate when you know that it will hurt you? Are you impatient with yourself when learning something new? Do you dislike some physical feature: your height, weight, hair, nose, etc.? Do you take your strengths for granted and harp on your weaknesses? Nothing hurts us more than not being accepted for who we are, and yet we do it to ourselves. Take your unloving behaviors and focus on one each day. On Monday, notice your strengths, on Tuesday accept your weaknesses, on Wednesday be more patient with yourself, on Thursday appreciate your physical features, and so on. Making these little changes can have a noticeable effect on your attitude, self-respect, and ability to nourish yourself with love. Even little changes have big effects over time, and you'll start to notice people reacting positively to your new outlook.

## Discover Your Lovable Qualities

Generally speaking, people have a very difficult time seeing themselves clearly, particularly the good things about themselves. To help with this, I like to have my clients write a list of their lovable qualities. Again, if you don't think you're lovable, how will others? This exercise is great to do with your spouse, where you contribute to each other's list of lovable qualities, but doing it alone is also fine. I'll walk you through it:

1. Both you and your spouse get a piece of paper and a pencil. Make three sections on your page: one that's titled "Me," (this should have the most space under it), another that's titled with your spouse's name, and a third that's titled "Me 2."
2. Think of three lovable qualities you possess and write those down under the "Me" heading.
3. Next, think about your spouse's lovable qualities, and write three of them down under the second heading.

4. Under the final "Me 2" heading, I want you to think of your friends and family. What are three lovable qualities they might say you have? Perhaps they've told you what they find lovable about you.
5. Once you've finished filling out your page, share what you wrote under your "Spouse" heading with your partner. Each of you should add these qualities to your "Me" page with your list of lovable qualities. You each should now have nine lovable qualities under your "Me" heading.
6. Slowly read your nine lovable qualities to your spouse. When you finish, see if you can remember each other's.

Continue adding to your list of lovable qualities by asking friends and loved ones what they love about you. We have this terrible habit of focusing only on the negative, which sabotages relationships, sabotages life and surely sabotages love. Start to change your perspective, silencing that negative inner voice by giving thanks for all of your lovable qualities and those of your spouse, and try to remember each other's list when you get upset or annoyed.

## Self-Reflection: Making Time for You

Seeing and evaluating our own behavior has become the very last thing we want to do, and yet to love ourselves we have to become the foremost students of "us." We have to study and be honest about our behavior, taking responsibility for all of it—the good and the not so good. Explanations for why we behave in certain automatic, unloving ways are okay, but they don't let us off the hook. We are still responsible for our behavior and the effect it has on others and ourselves. We may not like what we see, but loving ourselves means we can commit to learning new behaviors. Instead of using our energy to defend and explain our actions, we use that same energy to slowly, consciously substitute more loving behaviors toward others and ourselves.

A large part of this work includes accepting yourself, understanding yourself, believing in yourself, and forgiving yourself. This is extremely important, as loving yourself is the necessary foundation enabling you to persist toward your relationship objectives even when there are setbacks. If we don't love ourselves we self-sabotage, become impatient, and blame others and ourselves during frustrating circumstances. Becoming aware of our weaknesses is something we usually shy away from, since we are often at a loss for how to manage them. But without being clear about our weaknesses, we can't love ourselves fully, because in a sense, we're denying a part of who we are. Get to know your weaknesses the same way you get to know your strengths – by looking inside yourself and by asking loved ones, and remember that accepting your weaknesses is a sign of strength and a critical part of your personal growth.

# Chapter 3
# The Modern Marriage: Challenges and Expectations

The marriage relationship is unique, containing an overwhelming amount of shared experience. Even if you are an only child, like me, you are not going share as much of your daily life with a parent as you do with your spouse. Marriage by nature involves constant discovery, some good and some bad, all of which requires continual adjustment. Each of us is in an on-going growth cycle intellectually and emotionally, and the result is that the person you date is different than the person you marry, and the person you are on your wedding day is very different than the person you will be 25 years later. Your needs and expectations change through the years, and the person who's meant to fulfill them changes, too.

Decades ago, there were many external forces keeping marriages intact, including social and religious pressures. Times have changed, and instead of the external forces that kept marriages together, today we get "advice" from friends and the media. The messages from both these sources often urge people who are not happy in their marriages to separate and find happiness elsewhere rather than inspiring the couple to seek solutions. They tell us that it's ok to take the easy way out, walk away, and not put the work in. They feed a fantasy that we're better than what we've got, that we deserve more, that, "You could get a someone new tomorrow. John doesn't know how lucky he is. He'll be sorry when you walk out and will be begging you to come home."

## Don't Be Fooled by Their Smiles

We constantly compare ourselves to our peers, fostering couple jealousy that can poison marriages. We see that some people are seemingly perfectly happy in their marriages (which is often more public display than reality) and we feel that something must be wrong with our relationship or spouse. Toxic thoughts creep in when we're around other couples, like, "Susan doesn't appreciate me. She's constantly nagging me—not like Mike's wife, always bragging about how he fixed the car or put up the backyard fence." The effect is emotional exhaustion that stops people from trying their best to make their relationship work.

Don't be sucked in, and don't compare your relationship to what others advertise for public consumption. Just focus on finding the answers that will make *your* relationship better. An exercise that is very helpful to get out of the habit of comparing relationships and finding flaws is to make a list of the positive qualities of your spouse and relationship. Is there honesty? Dedication? Kindness? Willingness to share chores? Respect? Mutual interests? Once people make these lists they find that there are a lot more positives than negatives in the relationship. Armed with that knowledge, it becomes much easier to pinpoint the sore spots and work on them with a positive mindset.

Tell your spouse something you appreciate about them. Write in a journal about your favorite memory with your spouse, or about something you're looking forward to experiencing together in the future. Most importantly, try to become more aware of when you start comparing your relationship and your spouse to others so you can override that destructive pattern with positive, affirming thoughts. For example, "We are a hard-working, honest, fun-loving couple. We never went to relationship school, but we're trying our best and are now committed to enriching our marriage with these new tools."

## The Tyranny of Expectations

People get married for lots of different reasons: because it's a natural next step in a committed relationship, because their parents expect it, because their religion, culture, or society has taught them it's part of adult life, because it makes sense for financial or legal reasons, and most often because they're in love and want to build a life together. The underlying similarity is that they all believe that marriage will improve their lives and bring them happiness. People enter marriage with the highest hopes and best of intentions.

Even the traditional marriage vows don't contain the unconditionally loving component we need so much. "For better or worse, through sickness and health, till death do us part," asks couples to stick together through the worst circumstances life can throw at them. It doesn't say anything about promising to love one another unconditionally throughout those circumstances. The reason we all declare these vows is because we all assume that unconditional love, the vital component, comes bundled with this package. Most people believe that marrying someone who is caring and fun during the dating and engagement period, someone they love and who loves them, means that the sense of peace, acceptance and love they feel will last. We are not only full of hope that these wonderful feelings and behaviors will last a lifetime; we are *convinced* that they will.

## Did You Skip Relationship School?

It's not that we're naïve or deluded: we know relationships take work. When you sit down with people and have a serious conversation about marriage, even engaged couples will tell you that marriage isn't easy. They've seen their parents or friends struggle, and we're all familiar with the gloomy divorce statistics. In spite of the ability to intellectually recognize the challenges and realities of a lifelong commitment, another part of us is really in control, and that is the heart. The heart listens to the brain's logic and says, "Yes, but we'll be one of the couples that makes it." Love is optimistic, and couples think that they can avoid the mistakes they see others making, the mistakes they made in their past relationships, and prevent creating the same dysfunctions that their parents and relatives may have modeled for them.

As a therapist, I was curious to know what people really expected out of their marriage—why they decided to take the plunge knowing the statistics. My organization, The Human Development Company, interviewed hundreds of people—married, divorced, and engaged, both first timers and remarried. Here are some of the main expectations and reasons people gave as to why they chose to get married:

1. Companionship
2. Children
3. Create a home
4. Security – both financial and emotional
5. To feel normal (cultural)
6. Available sex
7. Have someone to grow old with

As it turns out, most couples do in fact get the seven items on this list. From the moment they marry, now they have a companion, a consistent sex partner, can plan for a home and children, have security, feel normal, and have someone they can grow old with. But even though people get what they expect, what they think they want, half of them still get divorced. So what's missing?

There has to be something more people yearn for, on a deeper level, which they only become aware of when they start to feel restless, unhappy, or break up. It's only when they think about what went wrong that they realize what was really missing.

| | |
|---|---|
| Inner Peace<br>Independence/Interdependence<br>(NOT dependence)<br>Authenticity; be allowed/<br>encouraged to be ourselves<br>Respect<br>Compassion<br>Consideration<br>Acceptance<br>Appreciation<br>Communication<br>Understanding<br>Encouragement<br>Etc. | =<br><br>**Being Loved**<br><br>Unconditionally |

Everyone I've worked with lets out a big sigh after hearing this list. We all yearn for these things, yet we cannot attain them unless we give and receive love unconditionally. This is what the fragile, hurting, childlike being inside all of us is calling out for: the unconditional love that we believe will heal our pain, fears, loneliness, or insecurity.

People genuinely believe that the close, loving bond of marriage will heal or mask their past hurt, and prevent future pain. We're all familiar with the concept of the honeymoon period. For many it's euphoria not unlike that of a starving man who finally found a consistent source of delicious food. Why shouldn't this feeling of being loved unconditionally persist as long as we're with this wonderful person we're dating? The problem is, people don't go to relationship school. They've never been taught how to unconditionally love another person—especially when problems arise, which they inevitably do. Now, the person we've chosen to trust with our hearts, the one who used to be so unconditionally loving with us, has hurt us.

Whether it was intentional or not, the result is the same: the illusion is shattered, and we're left facing our fears and pain alone— or so it seems to us. We're disillusioned, frustrated, and anxious. Since we usually aren't able to pinpoint our own source of pain (or even acknowledge that we are in pain) a sense of confusion lingers and grows more frustrating as time passes. It is this nagging sense of underlying frustration that makes us irritable and discontent, spilling over into our marriage. It's not that we expect our partners to read our minds, it's that we don't understand the source of our own dissatisfaction, or how to heal ourselves. We've never been given the tools or taught how to use them—until now.

# Chapter 4

# Your Marriage Toolkit:
# Use It or Lose It

Even marriages that are happy, fulfilling, and respectful go through rough spots and uncomfortable moments. We all need the essential tools to help us love one another unconditionally: awareness, vision, communication and unconditionally loving behavior. Next, we'll focus on developing these tools and applying them so that you can give and receive unconditional love in your relationships. It's important to remember that these tools are designed to be used holistically and sequentially—as you'll see, effective communication is impossible without a clear vision, just as a functional vision is impossible without awareness.

Throughout this chapter, I'll be sharing the story of a couple that came to me for help working through a rough patch in their relationship. As you read snippets of their story to see how they acquired and developed their relationship tools, spend a few moments thinking about how you would act in their situation. Then, when you're finished reading the book, I encourage you to see how your answers have changed.

## Francine & Larry

Francine and Larry had been happily married for over ten years. One day Francine started to feel like she just wanted to be alone. She became quiet and interacted as little as possible with Larry. Take a few moments and give the following questions some deep, heartfelt consideration. Imagine yourself in their situation.

What do you think Larry was thinking and feeling?

What do you think Francine was thinking and feeling?

What would you do if you were Larry?

What would you do if you were Francine?

Without having a vision for the marriage, without understanding the necessity and power of communication, and not knowing how to love unconditionally, the tools we'll be learning here, Francine and Larry drifted apart. She was busy with the children and he with his business. When they came to me they were very sad, convinced that they no longer loved each other.

What do you think?

If you were Francine or Larry's friend, how would you try to help them?

## Awareness: The Foundation of Conscious Behavior

Awareness is like a muscle that needs development. Centuries ago, the Chinese upper class used to bind girls' feet to make them look more feminine, which permanently damaged the muscles and bones. As adults, these women could barely walk—they certainly couldn't run, dance or perform athletics. The use of their feet was limited, and with it their enjoyment of life. Awareness can similarly be damaged when we are children, bound up by criticism, conditional love, impatience, discouragement, a lack of acceptance, or even by well-meaning parents who simply don't realize they're behaving conditionally and don't know how to develop a child's awareness.

Most psychotherapies, including Gestalt therapists, try to help people become more aware since it is the foundation for interacting with the world. A developed inner awareness pays attention to your physical and emotional inner state, and it tells you when things don't feel right in a relationship. Your awareness also establishes two important parameters: where you are, and where you want to be. Without awareness of your situation and how you feel about it, you can't begin to consider what you want, how to get it, or if you are even heading in the right direction.

It's equally important to become aware of your own actions and their effect on other people. For instance, you may not even realize you are doing something unloving while you are doing it. One indicator that can help you become more aware of these actions is noticing the other person's reaction to your behavior. Do they snap? Mutter defensively under their breath? Tear up and leave the room? Not call or answer the phone for days or weeks? To have close relationships we first have to commit to paying close attention to the way others react to our behavior and take it to heart.

Instead, often our tendency is to call someone too sensitive or to defend our own behavior. As you develop your awareness you will have the ability to evaluate your own motives/behaviors and consider the effect you will have on the other person before you speak or act. How often has something slipped out of your mouth and you immediately thought, "Oh…." It happens to me at times, but at least now I can notice, be understanding of the other person's reaction and can easily say, "I'm sorry, that came out wrong."

*"The best time to love with your whole heart is always now, in this moment, because no breath beyond the current is promised."*

-Fawn Weaver

## Building Awareness

How do you define love? What is your spouse's definition of love? I'll bet you haven't really discussed it—perhaps you never sat down to really think about it yourself—but it is one of the main causes of friction. We not only expect our spouse to automatically know our definition of love and the expectations that follow, we actually expect them to have the very same definition and expectations as ours. What a recipe for discord and disaster! Let's explore these issues and do a few pointed exercises that will start to bring some clarity to what your definitions of love are and how they color your expectations. Here are some examples of my clients' expectations based on their definitions of love:

| Client 1 | Client 2 | Client 3 |
|---|---|---|
| • Remembering birthdays | • Being affectionate, respectful and appreciative | • Sharing responsibilities |
| • Keeping holidays | | • Spending quality time with each other and the kids |
| • Buying gifts | • Patience, acceptance and understanding | |
| • Being courteous | | |
| • Going on vacations | • Communication | • Being authentic |
| • Calling regularly to check in | • Being thoughtful, considerate and kind | • Forgetting little things; forgiving big things |
| • Controlling one's temper | | • Intimacy |
| • Willingness to help | | • Accepting each other's family |

As you can see, each person had a very different understanding of love: for some it was certain actions or gestures, for others it was the quality of behavior, and for others it was a combination of both.

Using the space below, write what your own definition of what love is in the first column (you can extend the list to be as long as you want). In the second column, have your partner write his or her definition.

| My Definition of Love | My Partner's Definition |
|---|---|
|  |  |
|  |  |
|  |  |
|  |  |
|  |  |
|  |  |
|  |  |
|  |  |
|  |  |
|  |  |
|  |  |
|  |  |
|  |  |
|  |  |

Becoming aware of your expectations and those of your partner is a critical step in being able to make each other feel loved and cherished.

### Francine & Larry

Francine and Larry each spent some time developing their awareness. Francine began by considering what she was already aware of: the fact that she felt unhappy about getting older and uncomfortable in her own skin, as well as the fact that she viewed this as being a personal problem that she needed to deal with on her own. As she deepened and expanded her awareness, she realized that her sense of needing to deal with the problem on her own made Larry feel unloved. What she initially thought was a personal problem she began to realize was negatively affecting her husband and her marriage.

Meanwhile, Larry began by focusing on what he was currently aware of: his sadness that Francine was pulling away from him, his hurt that she wasn't showing him affection, and his frustration that she would not communicate with him about it. As he deepened his awareness, he realized that his frustration was slowly turning to resentment—which was getting in the way of them reconnecting and working through the problem together.

Finally, Francine and Larry were able to work on their shared awareness. They became aware of the fact that there was a solution to their problem, and that they each had an underlying sense of hopelessness that was preventing them from having a breakthrough. With all of this newfound awareness, they were able to create effective Visions to actively mend and strengthen their bond.

## No Vision, No Change

Have you ever run out of a few essential items, grabbed your car keys and gone to the supermarket? I have, and I came home with three things I didn't need and managed to forget the very items I needed to buy in the first place. Frustrated, I had to turn around and go back. When some people need to replenish their cupboards they do it thoughtfully. They take inventory, look on each shelf, make a list, and have a much better chance of coming home with all the right items than the person who did a quick mental inventory.

When most of us hear the word "vision," grand accomplishments come to mind: Martin Luther King Jr.'s vision of racial equality, or Kennedy's vision of landing on the moon. Vision implies that we see our goal very clearly, almost to the point of being able to hold it in our hand—like an architect's draft, or a business plan, crystal clear and very thorough. Visions require that we take time to think about what we want to create, write it down in detail, and persist until it's achieved.

Have you ever written a vision for any of your relationships? Most people think that sounds funny, and yet that is exactly what is missing from many struggling or unsatisfying relationships. The most pervasive reason relationships can become aimless, disappointing, and unfulfilling is because they lack a conscious vision to direct our actions and choices.

Consider how you approach each day. Do you jump out of bed with a tune on your lips or do you have to drag yourself out of bed? If it's the latter, chances are your enthusiasm is near zero and you are anticipating a day full of nothing but headaches, lingering problems or troublesome people. You need gallons of coffee just to autopilot through your day. Perhaps you'll simply choose to avoid the issues, leaving them to fester and stink up the next day.

# The Choice is Yours

All of this *sturm* and *drang,* the drama in relationships and life, is primarily because of a lack of thoughtful vision. Nobody's life is perfect, but what if your vision for each day was to be productive, have fun, address any problems head on, do your best and trust that everything will work out? What if you had a similar vision for your relationship? "I love my wife, and she loves me. I appreciate her strengths and accept her flaws, just as she appreciates and accepts mine. I feel at peace because we know how to listen and talk to each other about anything that may come up."

Some people might think this sounds ridiculously simple: create a vision and problems disappear. No, the problems don't disappear, but your approach to handling them changes. When your approach changes, you have a calm confidence that affects others, encourages compromise, leaves a lot of energy for constructive, positive creativity and leaves you with sufficient motivation to persist until a problem is resolved.

Have you ever seen the Bill Murray film *Groundhog Day?* It's about how our Vision for life, starting with our vision for each day, affects our experience. Bill Murray's character finds himself reliving the same day—February 2—over and over again. It feels like a curse. At first he becomes incredibly frustrated, stuck in a loop where nothing he does matters, and he eventually slips into bitterness and depression. He thinks up a different way of ending his life each day, only to wake up the next morning having to start all over again.

Then, his Vision changes, and he decides he can use the endless amount of time he has to learn and do good around the community: rescuing a boy who falls out of a tree, taking piano lessons, saving a man from choking on his dinner, and learning French. This leads him to build relationships with the people in his community. By the end of the film he has enriched his life, fallen in love, and broken the Groundhog Day curse. The key to his ultimate success was transforming his Vision for each day from cursing it to realizing that great possibilities exist. Enjoying life starts with having loving relationships, and those require thoughtful Visions. A thoughtful plan for growth, healing, and loving relationships is worth taking time to create.

Remember that, although a written Vision is necessary for organization and resolve, it is a living plan that is subject to change and growth. It becomes a feedback loop: as we begin to work with our Vision, we encounter setbacks, learn more about ourselves, and see the effects our new behaviors have on others. This creates a greater awareness of our relationships and our own needs, which we can then use to revise and improve our Visions. The cycle continues as our Visions continually evolve and help us reach our true goals.

## Feedback Loop

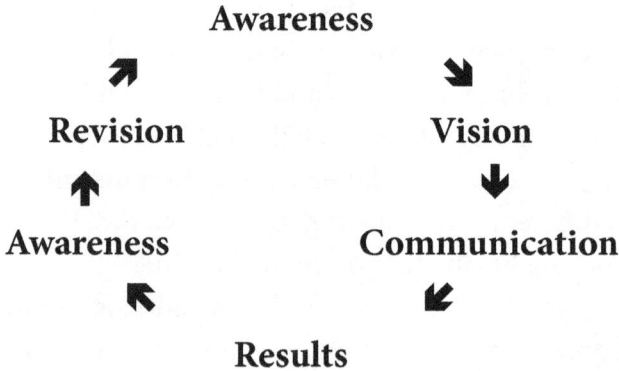

**Awareness**

**Revision**          **Vision**

**Awareness**          **Communication**

**Results**

### Francine & Larry

Francine and Larry had only one vision directing their behavior; "For better or worse, in sickness and health, till death do us part." Unfortunately that only kept them together but did not give them ways to turn their situation around. Like almost every other couple on Earth, they never created a written vision for their relationship. Visions drive behaviors and choices and without having a vision they just kept repeating the same behaviors over and over. Many couples feel trapped in the marriage, when actually they are trapped in their own limiting behaviors.

One of the first things we do when couples seek counseling is have them write a vision. It includes everything they can think of that they want from their spouse and the marriage.

What do you think Francine and Larry should include in their vision?

## Crafting a Dynamic Vision

How do we create a Vision that encompasses the constant changes and fluctuations of a marriage relationship? For starters we need to focus on the things that will never change. Both you and your spouse will always require the other to behave lovingly and unconditionally.

Secondly, you both will always need to feel heard. So, your Vision is that throughout the marriage you will both cultivate, awareness, loving behaviors and communication skills, which together will help you to work through any issues that may come up. When communication is effective and you're living with someone who loves you unconditionally, there is nowhere else that you want to go. Even major life changes or challenges will be handled in a way that a solution that keeps the marriage strong will eventually present itself.

Each of you may want to sit down and write your own individual Visions for the marriage; for example, your Vision of the kind of husband or wife you want to be. Invest some real time and thought into your Vision, and revisit it. Then, you can sit down together and create a shared Vision for your marriage, including what each of you need from each other but is not fully available yet.

It's so important to remember that Visions are living documents. Keep talking about your shared marriage Vision and keep revising it, particularly during milestone moments. Update it when you have children, when you buy a house, when you relocate, when you change jobs or take on different career roles, when you become empty nesters, and when you retire. Don't let it collect dust; like any living thing, your marriage Vision needs attention and care.

*"Success in marriage does not come merely through finding the right mate, but through being the right mate."*

-Barnett Brickner

# Spouse 1: Personal Relationship Vision

Take a few moments and create a vision for the kind of spouse you want to be. What qualities, habits, and attitudes do you want to bring to your marriage?

_____

_____

_____

_____

_____

_____

_____

_____

_____

_____

# Spouse 2: Personal Relationship Vision

Take a few moments and create a vision for the kind of spouse you want to be. What qualities, habits, and attitudes do you want to bring to your marriage?

_____

_____

_____

_____

_____

_____

_____

_____

_____

_____

# Spouse 1: Vision for Relationship Needs

Take a few moments and think about what you need from your spouse in order to feel unconditionally loved. What qualities, habits or attitudes do you want him or her to bring to your marriage?

_____

_____

_____

_____

_____

_____

_____

_____

_____

_____

# Spouse 2: Vision for Relationship Needs

Take a few moments and think about what you need from your spouse in order to feel unconditionally loved. What qualities, habits or attitudes do you want him or her to bring to your marriage?

_____

_____

_____

_____

_____

_____

_____

_____

_____

_____

_____

# Joint Vision for Your Marriage

Sit down together and devote some time to talking about how each of you envisions your marriage. What qualities, habits and attitudes do you want to establish in order for your relationship to thrive and grow? Which of your habits do you want to keep or further develop? What issues do you want to address or improve? Make this vision as complete as possible, and remember to revisit and revise your vision periodically.

_____

_____

_____

_____

_____

_____

_____

_____

_____

_____

*"Marriage is a commitment—a decision to do, all through life, that which will express your love for your spouse."*

-Herman Kieval

## Francine & Larry

Not surprisingly, Larry wanted more affection, more time, and much more communication. The fact that she wouldn't tell him what was going on for her made him feel that Francine stopped loving him, which she fervently denied. She felt that Larry was too busy with his work and friends, but was not asking him for more time or attention. She actually thought everything was OK with the marriage, and that the problem was her. She felt lost and confused and did not know where to turn for help. Larry felt disrespected and said that Francine's willingness to communicate with him would show respect and trust in him and their relationship. They created a very simple vision where the priority was communication, followed by affection.

What do you think about this vision?

Would you have included other elements?

Is there a little issue in your marriage that has lingered for too long, that could use a vision to resolve it?

## Communication: The Lifeblood of Relationships

Relationships are not static entities. As much as you may think that things are pretty much the same as they were five, ten, or fifteen years ago, they aren't. Relationships either slowly spiral in a positive direction or slowly deteriorate. Because change happens so slowly, it's easy to believe that the relationship is ok. This false perception allows spouses to tolerate, get used to, or not even consciously notice negative changes. One morning a spouse wakes up to discover the other wants a divorce. This is one of the reasons why intentional, thoughtful communication is so important for healthy marriages.

When is the last time you and your spouse had a "state of the union" discussion? Do you talk about issues as they arise, or let them fester? I strongly encourage all my couples to ask one another these four questions on a regular, weekly basis:

- Are you happy with your life?
- Are you happy with our relationship?
- Are you happy with me?
- What can I do to help you to be happier?

Ultimately, some of the issues affecting marriages have little to do with the spouse. Work stress, health problems, financial worries and other external factors can affect personal stress and relationship health. How reassuring is it to know that you can create a life-support system in your spouse, someone who is always there to encourage you and even more importantly, to just listen?

Get into the habit of a weekly heart-to-heart and I guarantee it will become a time you will both look forward to. It will validate why you love each other so much: because you know you're there for each other not only in times of crisis, but will be there to support each other through the myriad of daily struggles that may seem like small potatoes.

Another wonderful marriage habit to cultivate is making lists of things you are thankful for. Being grateful takes the focus off of the things that aren't going well and reminds you how much more there is to be thankful for so you don't take them for granted. This new perspective also changes your mindset to help you use your energy constructively, rather than getting mired in negative thoughts that are draining the life out of you and your marriage.

Couples will do almost anything to avoid fights and confrontations, especially when they're afraid of seeming petty or overly sensitive. Most people think, "Shouldn't s/he know after all this time?" about their particular sensitivities and sore spots. The problem is, no one is a mind reader, and your spouse can't figure out what may be troubling you all on his or her own. If you love somebody, isn't it easier to tell him/her what you want or don't want than to get angry, pout, or withdraw?

One of the biggest complaints people have about communication is that so often it feels like griping. It can seem like other people repeat themselves over and over about something that upset them, and that they just can't let it go. Our response is usually something like, "How many times are you going to bring this up? You've said it twenty times already. I got it, I got it." No, you didn't. The number one rule in communication is that when someone feels heard—really understood—they will let go of the issue that is troubling them. If you find your spouse repeating themselves or harping on the same issue, you need to go into active listening mode. Say, "It seems like you don't feel that I heard you the first time. I'm sorry—let me make sure I really pay attention this time."

*"When you make the sacrifice in marriage, you're sacrificing not to each other but to unity in a relationship."*

-Joseph Campbell

## Francine & Larry

Very often people are puzzled by the idea of having to learn communication. Doesn't everybody know how to communicate? That is certainly how Francine and Larry felt. Yes we all know how to make sounds and form words. We know how to give and receive compliments. It is the other stuff that finds us at a loss. Effective communication implies that when problems are discussed they lead to an agreeable resolution, and actually bring two people closer together. When Francine and Larry discussed problems they usually ended up in an argument that made things worse not better. In a day or two things would blow over, but it definitely did not enhance the relationship. Like many of us, they were hesitant to even start difficult conversations. "It's small stuff, there is no need to be petty," was their explanation, but every time they did, a little more resentment piled up in the corners of their hearts.

If you were Francine and Larry and decided to sit down and have a heart-to-heart about drifting apart, where would you start?

## Sticks and Stones May Break My Bones, but Words Will Surely Kill Me

Long after bruises and broken bones have healed, we still remember someone's thoughtless or ill-advised comment. We must become much more conscious and aware of just how hurtful words and behaviors can be, and how those wounds may never completely heal.

How can we rectify this problem? One of the great tools is mirroring, which focuses on intentional communication and active listening. One of the reasons it's so effective is that it makes our desire to understand another person's needs very clear to them. That is the unconditional part of the equation. Unconditional communication means putting aside your personal agenda and focusing all your energy on the relationship—making sure the other person feels that you really care about hearing what they're saying.

Simply put, mirroring involves repeating word for word two to three sentences that one person says to another. It involves the person who has something he or she wants to communicate, called the "Sender," and the person who will be listening and repeating, called the "Receiver."

**Follow These Steps:**

1. Sit face to face in close proximity, and determine who is the sender and who is the receiver. The sender asks, "Is this a good time to talk?"
2. If not, both agree on a later time. If yes, the sender begins with, "I know you love me and you know I love you." Then, the sender adds a couple of positive adjectives that describe the receiver.

3. The sender then begins their message with two or three short sentences.

4. The receiver says, "What I'm hearing you say is, '_____'" and repeats the sentences verbatim. When finished, the receiver asks, "Did I hear you correctly?"

5. The sender gives a "Pass" or a "No Pass." If it's "No Pass," the sender repeats the sentences once more.

6. The receiver asks each time, "Is there anything more you would like to say about that?"

7. Continue until the communication is complete.

Take special note of the question the receiver needs to ask after repeating the communication and getting a Pass: "Is there anything more you would like to say about that?" When a doctor cleans a wound he doesn't just do half, leaving some dirt so it can get infected. Unfortunately, that is exactly what we often do when communicating during conflicts. We don't want to hear it, so we try to interrupt or stop it. It winds up leaving a lot of dirt in the other person's wound, which will fester and infect the relationship over and over again.

Mirroring is not designed as conversation. It short-circuits our propensity for responding automatically, and develops our ability to be thoughtful when communicating. Focusing on saying a few sentences at a time, so the receiver can really hear and repeat what is being said, forces the sender to slow down and actually think about what they're saying, as opposed to the high-speed rattling we tend to do when we're upset.

The receiver, by having to concentrate and remember what is being said, is better able to shut down their defensive inner dialogue, is less likely to interrupt or misinterpret what they are hearing, and is able to stay present to the sender. The sender feels heard, feels safe, and feels what they are saying is important to the receiver. Both are better able to remain calm and lower their mounting defensiveness and escalating emotions. The message is communicated more clearly and understood more effectively.

People always ask me how they apply mirroring in their relationships when they are the only ones who know about it and are practicing it. The good news is it only takes one person. If confronted or asked, "Why are you repeating everything I say?" you can explain, "I want to make sure that I hear everything you're saying. This helps me to respond more appropriately. I want you to know that you're important, and what you're saying is important to me."

Effective communication depends on two crucial components: knowing how to constructively express your anger instead of holding it in and reiterating your loving connection at the start of such communication. Expressing anger is usually perceived as healthy, but that can wind up being a slippery slope, especially if we don't know how to express our anger lovingly.

Here is a situation that shows you how a typical communication about hurt feelings can be delivered in a both a negative and then a positive way. Imagine being told, "You don't love me. You could have come with me to the ballgame, but getting together with your stupid girlfriends is more important to you than I am. You couldn't care less about me." How would you react to hearing that? How would you feel? Defensive? Angry? Incredulous? This is not only conditional behavior but it does not communicate the truth. It only communicates what may feel like the truth in the heat of the moment. People hate to be misrepresented, and statements like this almost always lead to a defensive counterattack.

Instead, imagine saying to your spouse, "I know you love me, but it didn't feel like it. It felt like your friends were more important to you than me when you chose to be with them instead of coming to the game with me. It hurt and angered me." Remember, acknowledging that your spouse loves you first and then letting them know you're hurt allows for the right emotional environment to discuss the issues and get positive resolution.

Whenever my wife got upset her solution was to give me the silent treatment. I tried to talk to her and resolve the problem, but what I didn't realize was that I kept coming to her with reasonable arguments to explain my side of things, not affection. It's very common for some people to focus on winning an argument or justifying their position rather than expressing affection and reestablishing the love present in the relationship.

Finally, we want compassionate communication to inspire the other person to seek growth. The need for communication is usually due to discomfort, or behavior you want to change. Much of our communication is about what we want, without considering the other person's needs. He or she is expected to understand your feelings and adjust his or her behavior to satisfy you. However, communication is most effective when its purpose is to support and inspire the other in the relationship. We all find growth difficult and need compassion to accomplish it.

### Francine & Larry

As you've learned, it's always best to start by reestablishing the heart and soul of the relationship. People are together because they love each other, and since they don't have the tools to deal with problems, disagreements, they get frustrated with the other person. That of course winds up sending the message, "I don't love you," which is not true. The truth is, "I am frustrated by my inability to effectively get across what is troubling me, and your inability to listen to me and help resolve my issue."

As soon as Francine and Larry said, "I know you love me, and you know I love you," to each other, it dissolved the fear of rejection. They realized they loved each other and could breathe again. They were able to really listen to each other and work together to resolve the problem.

The rest was just mirroring, with Francine explaining to Larry that she was feeling older and it made her feel badly about herself. She was afraid to say anything because she didn't want anyone to try and talk her out of her feelings. She didn't realize how much it was hurting Larry. He told her she was still beautiful and desirable in his eyes. While it took her a little while to accept that as truth, the cycle of distancing was broken, and healing was taking place.

Is there a little issue in your own life that has lingered for too long? An issue that mirroring and saying "I know you love me and you know I love you," to each other might begin to resolve?

## Loving Unconditionally

The dating and courtship process is full of unconditional behavior. When a relationship is new and fragile, both parties are always putting their best foot forward. They're more respectful, appreciative, understanding, patient, flexible, and so on—all loving behaviors—during these early stages of the relationship than after a few years of marriage. Since the relationship is unconditional in the beginning, both parties have every reason to believe it will continue being unconditional as time passes and the relationship moves from dating to engaged to married or living together.

Think back to when you first began dating and getting to know your spouse, and remember the first time you got sick. You cancelled dinner plans because of your terrible cold and instead of getting frustrated or angry, your partner rushed over with something warm to eat, cold medicine, and a stack of movies. He or she took care of you, not minding that you looked a mess, wrapped up in an unflattering bathrobe with used tissues falling out of your pockets, and not worrying about your contagious germs. They were utterly unconditional with you.

But now that you're married, the moment your spouse says, "I think I'm coming down with something," you take five steps back. Catching a cold means one of you sleeping on the couch to avoid catching the bug and comments like, "Ugh, why can't you throw your disgusting tissues in the trash? They're all over the house!" This doesn't mean that your partner loves you any less now than he or she did before, in fact their love for you has likely grown and deepened as your relationship progressed. But once the relationship gets more secure and each of you feels more comfortable, automatic, conditional behaviors start to creep back in and replace the conscious, unconditional responses we were spoiled with at first and now rightly expect and deserve.

## The Keys to Remain Loving During Conflict

The exercises that follow are intended to help you get in touch with how it feels to turn off the flow of love, give you an opportunity to practice staying in unconditional mode, and see how the processes can be used in your marriage to love unconditionally even in upsetting situations. Without doing the exercises below in a heartfelt manner, and ultimately applying them, no amount of wisdom or stimulating information will affect your ability to love unconditionally. You need to practice. Please take a few moments to imagine that what is happening in these exercises is happening to you. Put yourself fully into each situation, carefully become aware of your feelings and picture your reactions.

The examples will demonstrate the typical ways spouses go into conditional mode with each other that must be unlearned. What is in the way for most people is pride, fear, or both. Pride screams, "I am right!" Fear begs not to be rejected. Instead there has to be a desire to stay connected and in unconditional mode. There are two effective scenarios you can learn for handling every upsetting situation. Process A is for when you're the one that's upset or angry. Process B is for when your spouse is upset or angry. These two processes can be applied to a myriad of situations. You have a chance to practice and learn them by applying them to exercises 1 thru 4. (Remember, reestablishing harmony is your primary aim, not being proven "right." The issues will resolve themselves once harmony is re-established.)

## Process A: You are the One Who's Upset

Step 1: Keep from walking away or shutting down
Step 2: Take your partner's hand
Step 3: Look in his/her eyes
Step 4: Acknowledge that you love him/her and that there is a problem
Step 5: Ask him/her if s/he knows why you are upset, then listen and mirror his/her point of view
Step 6: Communicate your issue and point of view patiently and lovingly

## Process B: Your Spouse is the One Who's Upset

Step 1: Ask him/her to stay if s/he starts to leave
Step 2: Ask to take your partner's hand
Step 3: Look in his/her eyes
Step 4: Say, "I know you're upset and I want to talk about it. I love you. I am sorry if I upset you."
Step 5: Listen and acknowledge his/her point of view
Step 6: Communicate your point of view compassionately

Practice applying Processes A and B to everyday situations and disagreements by taking yourself through the following examples:

1. You upset your spouse and just had an argument about it. Instead of talking it out s/he walks away from you. Close your eyes and think about what you feel. It's not a good feeling is it? Think about and become aware of what your past, automatic reaction has been,

then start to go through Process B. Ask him/her not to walk away, take his/her, hand, look into his/her eyes and without pride say, "I know you're upset and I want to talk about it. I love you. I am sorry if I made you upset and I know we can work this out. I would like to know how you feel about what just happened and then I will tell you how I feel. I would like to know what you would have done differently and I will tell you what I would have done. We can discuss this, both giving our opinions, until we come to an agreement. How do you feel about what just happened?"

Now imagine how your spouse feels when you walk away from him/her after s/he upset you. You're right; s/he feels the same way you did—badly. You have to be aware of the fact that you're hurting him/her when you walk away. Instead of walking away, use Process A to stay connected and unconditional.

How did you feel going through each exercise? Did you get a sense that resolution was possible using Processes A and B? Did it bring up more questions? Practicing with scenarios 2, 3 and 4 will help you find the answers.

2. You upset your spouse and you want to establish physical contact by holding his/her hand, but he/she moves away, or removes your hand from his/her shoulder or arm. How do you feel? Instead of your habit of accepting physical distance, how can you encourage an emotional environment in which your spouse welcomes your touch? Apply Process B and say without pride, "I know you're upset and don't want me to touch you. I love you. I am sorry if I made you upset." Then

say, "Please take my hand. I know we can work this out together." Continue with the rest of Process B.

Now imagine how your spouse feels when you don't allow him/her to touch you. S/he feels hurt, too. Now apply Process A. When you find yourself not wanting your spouse to touch you or recoiling from him/her, stop and try to become aware of what is generating that reaction. Remind yourself of the love you share and instead reciprocate by taking his/her hand. Then continue to follow Process A. How did it feel to work through the issue in a loving, connected environment?

3. You just upset your spouse, and instead of talking it out s/he starts yelling at you. You can't even get a word in. What do you feel? Instead of yelling over him/her or just shutting down and accepting this distancing behavior, how can you stop your spouse from continuing to yell and distance you? Turn to your spouse and say, without pride, "I know when you get upset that you raise your voice. You're probably not even aware that you do it, or how uncomfortable it makes me feel. I am sorry if I upset you. Please lower your voice or take a few minutes to cool off so we can discuss it." Continue with the second step and say, "Please take my hand," then proceed with the rest of Process B.

Put the shoe on the other foot and imagine how your spouse feels when you yell at them. Apply Process A so that when you find yourself yelling, stop and become aware of the automatic behaviors you fall back on. Instead say, "I am sorry for raising my voice," or, "I don't want to yell, so I need a few minutes to cool off." Then continue to follow Process A.

After doing the exercise you may be wondering how can you stop yourself or your spouse from yelling in the first place. The answer is that initially you can't do either. A person who is used to raising their voice will do it automatically and you can't respond until it happens. So in these scenarios, it is your response to yelling, either yours or your spouse's, and your own awareness of what triggers that response that will eventually create change and break the pattern of distance. It may be difficult to realize that the only thing you can really control is your own behavior, but remember that controlling your own reactions and responding with love will help your spouse to modify his/her own behavior, grow in his/her own awareness, and cultivate an unconditionally loving environment.

4. You just upset your spouse, and instead of talking and listening to your points s/he constantly interrupts you. How does this make you feel? How can you encourage your spouse to want to listen to your point of view rather than interrupt you? Again, apply Process B. The first step is to say, without pride, "I know you're upset and don't want to hear what I have to say. I love you. I am sorry if I made you upset." Continue through the rest of Process B.

Now imagine how your spouse feels when you constantly interrupt them. Apply Process A and when you find yourself interrupting, become aware of that tendency, its triggers, and make a conscious decision to stop. Say, "I am sorry for interrupting you." Continue follow through the rest of Process A.

How did it feel to choose to stay disconnected at the beginning of each exercise? Did you feel hurt, frustrated, confused, rejected, angry, sad, lonely, misunderstood, or anxious? Were these feelings added to whatever the original problem was? By going into conditional mode, as you can now see, the climate for resolving a problem can quickly deteriorate. In each example there was a problem, negative feelings were exacerbated by conditional behavior, and the conflict quickly escalated. But by using Processes A and B you can stay in unconditional mode, allowing the positive feelings to dissipate the negative. Did you see and feel how the environment changed? The changed environment is what encourages solutions.

The examples I've presented for staying in unconditional mode are aimed at overcoming the established patterns of distancing. Its effects from years of similar behavior may have already taken root and grown into a fixture in your relationship. Fortunately, brain research has discovered that there is hope; the patterns can be reversed. The neuropathways that guide our automatic behavior can be rewired with practice. Finding solutions requires your continued awareness and desire to stay in unconditional mode. So, practice Processes A and B until those behaviors take root and become the norm.

Painful feelings lead most people to try and forget about the problem. The adage, "Time heals all wounds," is applied to problems both small and large. But time alone doesn't heal at all. The hurtful feelings only accumulate and the eggshells we walk on continue to pile up. Going into conditional mode never solves the problem, but loving unconditionally by applying Processes A and B can prevent a problem from becoming a mess and building up in the first place.

# Chapter 5
# In Real Life: The Tools and Concepts at Work

In this chapter I will describe real-life situations that some of my clients faced and challenge you to consider how you would respond. Go through the whole process, using awareness, vision and communication. At the end of each story I'll explain how the conflict was resolved, but going through it on your own first gives you a chance to put what you've been reading into practice. When you are prompted, I encourage you to pause, consider what your approach would be and write down some of your thoughts before continuing.

## Betty and Jim

Let's look at an example of a marriage that's missing the tools it needs to succeed. A young woman we will call "Betty" was looking for love and marriage. Although friendly, bright and pretty, somehow finding the right person eluded her into her thirties. Then she met a very sweet, free-spirited young man named "Jim." Jim swept Betty off her feet, and they decided to get married. Jim was moving from one job to another, not quite finding himself. Betty, on the other hand, was making a name for herself in her field, achieving the commensurate titles and raises. Soon it was decided that Jim would stay home and take care of their young children. Although on paper this looked like the right decision, eventually conflicts arose.

Betty had become used to being an aggressive go-getter at work, and since she's a woman she had to push her ideas harder and be more persistent and assertive than usual. Once she got home, that was difficult to switch off. She found herself acting like the "boss" to her husband; she was unable to compromise, listen compassionately, or show appreciation to the extent that her husband needed.

Jim began to feel taken for granted, belittled, and neglected. In addition, he grew jealous of his wife's career success, her camaraderie with her co-workers, and the appreciation she received from the higher-ups for her innovative ideas, and started to want to go back to work and achieve those things himself. Friction arose in the marriage, and neither found themselves equipped with the tools they needed to understand the other's point of view and work through the problems. Conflicts arose about who was head of the household and who controlled money decisions. Left unresolved, these issues escalated.

Pause for a few moments and imagine yourself as either Jim or Betty. How would you address this conflict, using what you've learned about awareness, vision and communication? This is a good opportunity for you to put what you've read into practice before applying it to your own relationship. After you've taken a little while to go through the process yourself, I'll walk you through how I helped Jim and Betty repair their marriage and strengthen their bond.

*Take a moment to reflect on how you would approach this problem using the tools and ideas that you've learned.*

I spent a few sessions with Jim and Betty developing their awareness so they could make crystal clear the core issues at play and recognize their own needs and desires for their relationship. Once their eyes were open, the cure was to develop a new, thoughtful vision for the marriage. Although they were both skeptical about the value of a vision, they complied.

They each wrote their own vision first, then compared notes. To their surprise, they discovered they were in agreement in many respects: both wanted a nurturing, loving, supportive, and affectionate relationship. Discussing it made them realize that they had actually had that type of relationship in the past, and that there was no reason that with a little hard work they couldn't have it once again.

Next, they created a shared vision for their marriage, one they could own and work towards together. They discussed and agreed on parenting approaches, money habits, and spending quality time with each other. These areas caused most of their past conflicts and had never satisfactorily been resolved. After writing their vision for each area, with a bit of coaching and the realization that compromise was essential for progress, they arrived at a mutual vision each said they could be happy with. It's important to note that a strong, functional vision is generally one where both parties feel they had to give in or compromise more than they'd have liked.

Jim and Betty came to understand that communication and compromise were essential to realizing their vision, and that they wanted to make loving conversation a top priority in their marriage. For instance, they agreed that they would turn off the TV, laptop and smartphones after the kids went to bed and reconnect with one another. Jim would ask Betty how her day was, help her unwind, and then Betty would ask Jim about his day. They both listened with interest and appreciation. The three tools of awareness, vision and communication, as well as their inherent ability and desire to love each other unconditionally, won the day.

## John and Marlene

Let's look at another example. "John" is a hardworking craftsman who married and had three beautiful children. He had a job in the city, but it wasn't enough to allow his wife to stay home and take care of their young children. So, John got a second job working evenings and weekends in the suburbs. The second job paid much better than the first, and after a while John saved enough money to buy a family home. It wasn't in great condition, so little by little, with whatever money and time was available, John started to fix the house. As the years passed, it looked like all his hard work was paying off: the kids were doing well in school and planning to go to college, they had a beautiful family home, and John was proud of the fruits of his labor.

Throughout all this, his wife "Marlene" began to get restless and unsatisfied with how much time John spent away from home working. They started fighting about it, arguing more and more frequently. Marlene tried asking him to cut back to reasonable hours, but her approach was impatient, angry, and lacked an understanding of what John was trying to accomplish. John only heard accusations that he was an inattentive husband and father, instead of being appreciated for being a great provider. Angrily, John tried to explain to Marlene that since she didn't work, he would only be able to cut back on his hours once their girls were out of college. But Marlene only heard that her request was unreasonable and not an option.

Both John and Marlene got defensive, misunderstandings arose, communication stopped and the conflict spiraled until love was cut off on both sides. The situation festered and John and Marlene started to doubt each other's love. Encouraged by her friends, Marlene filed for divorce.

*Take a moment to reflect on how you would approach this problem using the tools and ideas that you've learned.*

John and Marlene started to address their communication issues by practicing the mirroring technique. It's very important to note that they started by discussing topics that were not nearly as contentious—whose turn it was to do the dishes, or whose movie pick they would watch that night—rather than the issue of John's work schedule. By practicing first with these smaller, less emotionally charged topics, they could focus on the technique without communication spiraling into an argument. Resolving these smaller issues also dissolved a lot of lingering resentment, which was always a major sore spot in the relationship and fed their larger issues.

Soon they were ready to discuss the core problem of John's work/life balance and Marlene's desire to have him home more often. Mirroring helped each of them to really listen closely to what the other was saying. They each realized that the other person often made sense, and that they didn't need to get defensive. As they took turns as the "Sender," they realized that truly feeling heard made them feel loved and understood, and brought them closer together.

Marlene realized that John needed to hear appreciation for his hard work, and John realized that his wife simply missed him and wanted more time together. They recognized that the issues came from very loving intentions on both sides. This revelation allowed them to work together as a team to create a plan: what would have to happen in order for John to be able to cut back his work hours? They created a tighter budget to eliminate needless spending on non-essentials, and they decided that Marlene could provide another source of income by getting a part-time job. Marlene had always liked retail and interacting with customers. She found a position after only a few weeks.

John and Marlene learned that trying to speak over each other without listening caused needless strife. Once they were willing to work together for the benefit of the marriage they were able to create solutions that made each of them happy. It made Marlene and John feel like they were a team, each contributing financially and creating a future together as a couple.

What's at stake here is mastery of life. No matter what we embark on doing we want to become as good at it as possible. It gives us great satisfaction to be really, really good at something. It also feels good to have people respond to that mastery, whether it is having a great sense of humor that is cultivated by watching comedies and trying out quips to amuse others, or being a good cook or baker by trying countless recipes, to playing an instrument.

Mastery requires time and practice, but produces real rewards, especially mastering the way we conduct ourselves and interact with others. Mastery means bringing the best out of yourself and others. It means feeling consistently good about yourself and helping others feel that way too. Loving yourself, being an effective listener and communicator, thinking before acting, particularly in relationships, and being aware of your and others feelings so as to respond always appropriately is, without a question, the ultimate gift anyone can give themselves.

The good news is that the ideas presented in this book have consistently been proven to work. That means that you now have tools and concepts, and the only missing ingredient is totally in your control—your own time and effort to practice and use what you have learned.

My organization, The Human Development Company, is here to help you on this magnificent journey. Go to our website www.thdc.org and join a growing community of couples and families learning and sharing new ideas about what makes love eternal.

# Chapter 6

# Watching Movies to Grow Closer Together

I want to leave you with a few additional exercises you and your spouse can do together to further develop your toolkit in a fun and productive way. A three-year study recently concluded that the divorce rate was cut in half for newlyweds who watched and discussed movies featuring couples dealing with common relationship issues.[1] The couples chose a movie from a list provided, and then answered a set of questions. I'd like to provide you with a similar exercise, with the questions tailored to reflect the theory and tools I've developed over the last 30 years.

Here's how it works: pick a movie from the following page (or choose your own), pop some popcorn, and snuggle up for a cozy night in. When the movie's over, look over and discuss the corresponding questions. So, dim the lights and let's get started!

[1] "Is skills training necessary for the primary prevention of marital distress and dissolution? A 3-year experimental study of three interventions." Rogge, Ronald D.; Cobb, Rebecca J.; Lawrence, Erika; Johnson, Matthew D.; Bradbury, Thomas N. *Journal of Consulting and Clinical Psychology*, Vol. 81(6), Dec 2013, 949-961.

### *Before Sunset* (2004)
Ethan Hawke and Julie Delpy

### *The Five-Year Engagement* (2012)
Jason Segel and Emily Blunt

### *The Money Pit* (1986)
Tom Hanks and Shelley Long

### *True Lies* (1994)
Arnold Schwarzenegger and Jamie Lee Curtis

### *This Is 40* (2012)
Paul Rudd and Leslie Mann

### *Gone With the Wind* (1939)
Clark Gable and Vivien Leigh

### *The Thin Man* (1934)
William Powell and Myrna Loy

### *Date Night* (2010)
Steve Carell and Tina Fey

## *Or Choose Your Own!*

# Questions for Thought and Discussion

1. What were the characters aware of in themselves and their partner? What were they unaware of?

2. How did each character's Vision (conscious or subconscious) affect their relationship? What Vision would you create instead?

3. Are the characters ever unloving or conditional with each other? In what ways could they be more loving/unconditional?

4. How do the characters handle conflict? Does communication break down? Do they stay loving? How does this compare to your relationship?

5. How do the characters communicate with each other? Do they ever blame each other or jump to conclusions? How does this compare to your relationship? How would you improve their communication?

6. Did each partner love themselves unconditionally? How did they struggle to balance loving themselves and loving their partner? How does this compare to your experience?

7. Did each partner seem to have similar expectations for the relationship? Were they open about their expectations with each other? How does their experience compare to your relationship?

# About the Author

Stefan Deutsch is the founder and president of The Human Development Company, an educational, not-for-profit organization that focuses on human development. He is the former founder and executive director of Impact on Hunger, Inc., which became the educational umbrella arm of the US hunger community, including UNICEF.

Deutsch is a certified Gestalt Psychotherapist. He hosted over one hundred weekly, one-hour, call-in radio shows on human development, love and relationships, and his guests included authors, healthcare professionals, and executive directors of various women's groups, child care facilities and senior centers. He also took calls from listeners seeking relationship advice and personal counseling.

Deutsch has presented his human development theories at major conferences and workshops around the globe, including the 2012 International Conference for the Association for the Advancement of Gestalt Theory, the 2011 International Conference of the Society for Psychotherapy Research, and the 2010 Society for the Exploration of Psychotherapy Integration. He has published articles in major publications, including *New Therapist*, *Body Psychotherapy*, *Parenting*, and *Creations* magazines, and has served as the resident expert on marriage, relationships and parenting for websites including LongIsland.com and LIWeddings.com.

# About The Human Development Company

The Human Development Company is an educational research organization built on The Continuum Theory™ of Human Development, a superordinate theory of lifespan that gives a clear roadmap to developing the innate potential of every human being. THDC staff consists of highly educated professionals working on several diverse applications of Stefan Deutsch's theory of love and human development, including:

1. *Saving A Marriage – Saves A Family* is a national campaign to reduce divorce in America 20% by the year 2020. Divorce rips families apart; creates emotional hardships for children from which many never recover; creates financial hardships; disrupts a child's ability to thrive in school; and beyond. Live events are given free of charge for engaged and married couples to teach them the tools they need to safeguard their marriages.
2. SELFS is a K-12 school curriculum based on a new model of human development that focuses on teaching students, parents and teachers awareness, vision, communication and unconditional behavior.

3. A student-led university and college resident life program that promotes self-esteem, interpersonal relationships, and unconditionally loving behavior.

4. A psychotherapist training program introducing Deutsch's unique approach to helping patients heal themselves and their significant relationships.

5. Teaching parents to do the one thing they are sure they do, but unintentionally do not: be unconditionally loving, even when the young child, teenager, or adult child disappoints, hurts, or angers them.

6. Initiatives to help the baby boomer generation perceive the aging process as one of power and promise, rather than decline. He coined the phrase LifePros© to describe such aging individuals.

Prior to founding The Human Development Company, Stefan Deutsch co-founded Impact on Hunger, Inc., which became the educational arm of the entire US hunger community, including UNICEF. Impact on Hunger produced the first hunger education curriculum for grades K-12, funded by AID. Its projects included Patrick's Walk, an endeavor that was blessed by the Pope, a two-year partnership campaign with Muhammad Ali, and the U.S.'s first food collection "Hunger Awareness Day" at the NY Mets Shea Stadium.

In time, Deutsch came to understand that Impact was attacking the symptoms of hunger, not the source. He determined to address the root cause of hunger, depression and unhappiness, and his theoretical research led him to conclude it was our inability and fear of loving ourselves and others unconditionally that prevented human beings from reaching their full potential. With this perspective, it becomes impossible to witness others' physical or emotional hunger, or be complicit in their exploitation, disenfranchisement, and disempowerment.

Over the past 10 years, Deutsch has given talks and workshops for singles, couples, parents, seniors and therapists. Now, THDC teaches human beings how to become self-sufficient when it comes to loving themselves, empowering them to love others unconditionally.

The Human Development Company is always looking to connect with those who are interested in its theories and approaches. If you are interested in learning more about THDC or becoming involved with one of its programs, visit www.thdc.org for more information and to connect with a program director.

www.ingramcontent.com/pod-product-compliance
Lightning Source LLC
Chambersburg PA
CBHW032153020426
42334CB00016B/1272